CRACKING
THE RESISTANCE
—CODE—

How to Break Through Fear of
Uncertainty and Write Your Book

DAWN MONTEFUSCO

CRACKING THE RESISTANCE CODE

Copyright © 2022 Dawn Montefusco

Book Design by
Transcendent Publishing

ISBN: 979-8-9868507-6-4

Printed in the United States of America.

for Jenna Roberts

Contents

A word after a word after a word is power.
–Margaret Atwood

Preface

No matter how many times I do it, there is a discomfort in writing that is hard to explain. I think the best way to describe it is to think of the creative process as a consistent twisting beyond a comfort zone, like stretching in yoga or attempting to sit still in meditation. I think if we're not slightly uncomfortable while writing then we're probably not reaching our potential. So how do we allow ourselves to step into the uneasiness of the arena over and over instead of sitting in the comfort of the bleachers?

I always find it funny when a client wants to know exactly how their book will turn out before they've even written a word of it. If that were possible to know – which it isn't – they would be missing out on one of the great joys of writing: the mystery, the battle and the conquest of breaking through to see what's on the other side. A writer must accept living with uncertainty. You'll never know what you are about to write until you write it.

The choices are myriad, the outcomes always unforeseeable. We do what we can to create the illusion that we are in control of the process, but we rarely are. This is also a meditation on how to live your life. We are all living a mystery.

What I've learned after two decades of writing, teaching and coaching is that there is no way to avoid the discomfort of self-doubt and fear that comes with writing. These negative thoughts and feelings can create so much resistance that many great writers never even get started. Sure, there are some that say it's no big deal, but I don't believe them. When prodded even writers who claim it's easy will admit to battling and conquering self-doubt.

I wrote this book hoping to inspire writers to become aware of their resistance so they can break through it and experience the joy of getting to the other side, which brings a deep sense of accomplishment.

At the end of each chapter, I've added questions or action steps to use as a guide to help you integrate this material. I highly recommend you take five minutes after each chapter to give inquiry to this in your life. It is through the written word and inquiry that makes it easier to transcend past our resistance.

Introduction

My childhood was in many ways the quintessential American story. My mother and father were both the children of immigrants – Mom's parents were from Warsaw, Poland and Dad's were from Naples, Italy – who had escaped the ravages of World War II by coming to the U.S. They settled in New York – that melting pot within a melting pot – and worked tirelessly to build a new life from the ground up.

The vibe in my home was one of deep gratitude, resilience, and love, but also fear. My grandparents knew the painful reality of having their countries of origin ripped apart by war. My parents faced the challenge of keeping me safe during the crime-ridden New York City of the 1970s and 80s, Survival meant learning street smarts, especially in the Bronx, where we lived and was at that time one of the most dangerous places in the nation. My Italian American father joined the civilian vigilantes helping the police manage the crime on the streets and subways. Dad, whose name was Frank, resembled a handsome Italian mobster (picture a cross between Al Pacino and James Dean). A tough guy with a compassion for justice. My cousin became a cop in Harlem. Everyone was determined that I, a young girl, would be able to safely make it to school and back each day. Indeed, by the age of ten I'd acquired some unusual survival skills. Not only did I learn how to carry myself and use body language that made me less of a target for predators, but I was also taught how to identify threats and control my fear when faced with gunmen, gang members or male predators. My dad was a loving father who wanted to protect his only child and he prepared me for every kind of emergency, assault, or dangerous situation. He showed his love by helping me learn how to survive.

I was taught how to break into house windows in case I got locked out, how to use a switchblade to open a door without a doorknob, how to use a safety pin to unlock doors or use a hammer to break open a master padlock if I forgot the code or key and had to get to something to use as a weapon. I was never a thief. I was taught these skills as a way to avoid or escape a violent assault or getting trapped in a fire (NYC fire codes often went unenforced at the time). Dad programmed me with a survivor's mindset and showed me how to crack codes mentally, emotionally, and figuratively; however, the most important code I was taught to crack was the psychological code of the mind when it went into fear or resistance.

"The mind is tricky," he would say. "It doesn't always know the difference between real danger and imagined danger. The thing you want to trust is below your neckline, your gut, and let your intuition guide you."

"How?" I asked one day as I sat on the couch with him. I was only thirteen at the time.

He turned to look me deeply in the eyes.

"You must learn to relax, never resist anything. It will give you the upper hand. You'll be able to figure out the vibe of any situation. When you relax you can use all of your senses," he said.

My dad also taught me that I could decide to be a victim – cower, cry, beg for mercy, and shrink – which is what every predator wants, or I could learn to bravely stand up tall, look them in the eye, and be ready to outwit my opponent in a variety of ways.

"But the number one rule is to trust your gut. Feel your way through life, avoid real danger. I'll teach you," he said.

Everything he taught me was based on his own experiences and the way in which he handled himself. He was tough, but he prided himself on never having to pull out the nine-millimeter he carried; he was trained in self-defense, but never liked to fight. Instead, he was a peaceful warrior, focused on the power of the mind. He taught me about inner chi, how to use my energy as a force to be reckoned with, and how to harness the power of my spirit and intuition. He showed me how to stay calm when I got nervous and why it's important to remember that with practice, we can also train our brain to navigate fear and doubt.

Among Dad's greatest gifts were his creativity and his ability to motivate. He was a poet and a writer, and though he was never published he gave me the courage to write and express myself through words. I never feared being a writer until I got older, when resistance crawled into my mind and took me as a slave. I'm so grateful for my father's teaching because, though he didn't realize it at the time, he was showing me how to crack the resistance code, and help other writers do it too.

If you want to write but feel stuck, maybe you beat yourself up or think you're not a writer, then this book is for you. I don't care how many times you've tried, or how many beginnings you have written, or if you've been writing in your journal and don't know what to do with it, or if you're twenty-five or seventy-five – you can still be a best-selling writer, a famous poet or songwriter. You can write whatever you desire. You can, with your words, make a big impact on the world. One thing I know for sure: we are born with dreams and aspirations for a reason, and if we don't follow through with them, we will never be fulfilled. I don't believe in a creator that would give us the desire to do something but not the tools to be successful doing it. If you are reading this, you *are* a writer! How can I be so sure? Because you didn't pick up a book on how to be an architect or a lawyer. You picked up this one, because you want – and you were meant – to write.

As we get older and move through a myriad of life experiences, we realize that we have the power to change and transform. Yet we've been conditioned to believe that we should have already fulfilled our dreams "by now." It feels like life is whizzing by, and social media makes us feel like we are always missing out on something. Perhaps you're thinking you should have traveled the world by now, or you should have had children, gotten married, or started a business – the list of shoulda, woulda, couldas is so long it's enough to stop you from doing anything because you should have done it already, right?

Wrong.

You didn't do it yet because it wasn't supposed to be done until now – and this is especially true of writing a book. Good writers are like good wine or a good stew – they get better as they develop more experiences, knowledge, and wisdom.

And here's another thing to keep in mind: This is the best time in all of human history to be a writer. Let me repeat that sentence – *This is the best time in all of human history to be a writer.* With social media and the internet at our disposal, there truly are no limits to being seen, heard, and read – no matter where we live or how much money we have. There is also a huge need for more content creators. With billions of consumers of books and only approximately 600,000 books coming out each year, we will always have an audience.

And yet, this wide-open field with endless opportunities seems to have created a paradoxical paralysis. In fact, I've found that more writers are suffering from resistance now than ever before.

Words can live in our heads and in our souls for years and then, when we sit down to put them onto the page, we're confronted with a crippling feeling that holds us back. Many writers are afraid to venture beyond that crippling feeling.

In the following pages I share what is really going on when you feel stuck. Though it may feel like an unbearable external force, it's really just an inside job, a code that accidentally gets embedded in your mind and tries to hold you back, sometimes creating a frustrating paralysis.

Here is what I want you to embrace: whatever you want to write must be written! It doesn't have to be a long book, or a traditional book. There are no rules anymore. Cracking your resistance code entails embracing yourself as a writer and a creator. As long as you are alive and reading this, it's not too late to be a bestselling writer in any genre: memoir, poetry, non-fiction, or fiction – you name it. It doesn't have to be a long book or take years. It can be a short book and take weeks.

Fear can hold you hostage temporarily, but regret lasts forever. Now is your time to write, so let's get cracking!

Questions / Thoughts for Inquiry

1. What book would you write if you knew it would be a guaranteed best seller? Dream big. Be unreasonable. Tell yourself the truth.

2. List five of your all-time favorite books, the ones you recommend to friends. See what they all have in common. Is there a pattern?

3. Write at least one paragraph about a time in your life that you did something you were afraid to do and it turned out great.

PART I

Know the Enemy

What is Resistance?

We've all heard of taking the "path of least resistance," which is another way of saying to take the easy way. The problem for writers is that creative pursuits inherently create resistance because they require us to take a leap into the unknown. No matter how well you've planned, outlined, and visualized you just never know what's going to come out until you open your channels of trust, start writing, and allow your spirit to guide you.

It's always been fascinating to me that we can understand something intellectually, philosophically, and even spiritually, but until we understand it experientially, we really don't know it. You can hypothesize about it, even teach it, but true learning comes when you are willing to experience it.

It comes as no surprise then that when I embarked on writing a book on how to help writers break through resistance, I experienced some of the greatest resistance to writing that I had ever encountered.

Indeed, for over a year after I announced the title of this book, I was plagued with fear, self-doubt, and anxiety. Every time I attempted to write I saw myself as a coward, an imposter, a liar, and a cheat. Eventually, though, I saw the twist that God wanted me to experience. If I were to help thousands of people out of resistance, I would first have to move through it myself.

I was *in* it. Neck deep. Stuck in the muck of imagined worst-case scenarios, and then I lost my ability to write. I went into the paralysis of analysis. I remembered my father's teaching: I could decide to be a victim, or I could build up the muscle and the bravery to outwit my opponent. The opponent was fierce: hard core resistance.

One thing I've witnessed and experienced is that the adult mind is always scanning for danger. It's the most annoying thing ever. This is due to the reptilian brain – or what I like to call the "mafia" part of the brain, located at the base of the skull. Its job is to protect us, and it takes this job very seriously, always looking for who or what's going to whack you and doing anything it can to keep this from happening. But here's the rub: anything that leads us into unknown territory is, by default, dangerous. Think about how it might feel to walk into a pitch-dark room in an unknown building. Scary, huh? You'd have to feel around with your hands, trying to make sense of where to go next. Every sound, every thought, every inch would have your imagination going wild with thoughts of danger. That's how the survival part of our brain interprets creativity: a scary, dark, unknown place.

As children, we have not yet learned that creativity is possibly dangerous. We are told to make a mess of things and enjoy the process. If we got it wrong, we could throw away our picture or mash the lump of Play-Doh and start over. We were *supposed* to make a mess and experiment with lots of ideas, and were told to just go for it without any pressure to do it right. We were, in fact, told that doing it "wrong" was how we discovered new things. Going back even further, no one tells a toddler who is trying to walk, "You should probably stop trying to walk and just crawl for the rest of your life." Instead, family cheers the toddler on with every fall and every step until one day they're walking.

I once heard a story about a professor who had a little five-year-old daughter. One morning, as he bent to kiss her goodbye, she asked, "Daddy, what do you do at work?" "I teach people how to draw," he replied. She looked at him in surprise. "You mean they forget?"

It is the same for writing. As children we are free to write and be silly, to use our imaginations without limitations, or spontaneously start singing, and make things up as we go.

Once we hit elementary school, however, they flip the script on us. Suddenly we have to conform to writing conventions and strive for external validation (i.e., good grades, penmanship or syntax) rather than pleasing ourselves and excited to experiment with new ideas. Then we start comparing ourselves to others – or worse, our teachers and parents making the comparisons. We start hearing things like art "won't pay the bills," and before we know it we've talked ourselves out of our greatest gifts and pick up something we hate to do because it seems like the "right" or "logical" move. This is what the path of least resistance looks like for creatives. We think that maybe our lives will get better if we fit in, please others, and try to forget what we really wished for. The horrible truth is that if a person is living the wrong life, they literally become the walking dead.

Another common saying is "Whatever you resist will persist," the idea being that when you fight or pretend something doesn't exist it only grows stronger. Fear begets fear and resistance generates more resistance. For writers and poets who let years or decades go by without putting their words to paper, the pent-up fear and resistance can lead to depression, anxiety, and even physical symptoms. Why? Because all those words, all those inspired ideas, are swirling through their minds with no outlet creating a chaotic mentally miserable landscape.

Let's look at some definitions of resistance:

- the refusal to accept or comply with something; the attempt to prevent something by action or argument

- armed or violent opposition

- a secret organization resisting authority

- the impeding, slowing, or stopping effect exerted by one material thing on another

- an opposing force

As you read this book you'll find (and may be annoyed) that I repeatedly say, "*Anything that keeps you from writing stems from resistance and fear.*" Keep in mind, though, that there is a difference between the two. Fear is natural, and when we take action in the face of it, we call that courage. Fear is not necessarily bad; for example, we can be afraid of fun things like rollercoasters and getting married, or a first kiss, or going to our first day of school. Resistance, on the other hand, is evil, diabolical. Resistance is truly out to get us because it wants to keep us "safe" and thus, immobile.

During the first six months of the pandemic shutdown in 2020, I thought I would get tons of writing done. Instead, I was stuck in a comparison loop. While hundreds of thousands of people jumped on social media to write and blog and tweet and tell stories, I sank into a soggy swampy imaginary landfill of insecurities. It was more like quicksand, because the harder

I tried to fight to get out of it the stronger the resistance became. I started to feel smaller and smaller. I started to feel insignificant. It was the first time in my life that I doubted my ability as a writer. Resistance was trying every trick in the book (pun *intended*) to shut me down.

Then I saw the cosmic joke. The man behind the curtain, just like in the Wizard of Oz. It was all an illusion. I was trying to stop myself because what if I succeeded? What if I won the war inside myself? What if I cracked the code? What would happen then?

That's the moment I found it – that magical path of trust – and that day I took my power back. I popped out of resistance and the shift took place in just about every area of my life. My spiritual channels unclogged, my body felt better, and my creativity was unleashed. I was writing.

"The best time to plant a tree is twenty years ago. The second-best time is now."

– Chinese Proverb

The message here is this: the length of one's life is not nearly as important as the experience. You cannot rewrite the past, but you can start now and chart the future you want. If you're stuck in resistance, read on. We are about to crack the code!

Questions / Thoughts for Inquiry

1. When you feel resistance where do you feel it in your body?

2. Describe the feeling of resistance. How much does it weigh? Does it have a color? Is it cool or warm? Does it vibrate or is it stiff?

3. What is your first memory of doing something that you were praised for as a child? It could be a drawing, a dance, a poem, riding a bike, walking, or anything that excited you and made you smile and feel joy about doing it?

The Meaning-Making Machine

Any great warrior or soldier knows that it takes hard training before you go into combat. The same is true when battling resistance, and the first step in this training is to become completely aware of your "meaning-making machine."

I first heard the term back when I was training to be a Transformational Solutions-Focused Life Coach, At Erickson College when I was thirty-five, and it truly changed everything for me. As soon as my teacher said, "The brain is a meaning-making machine," I immediately recognized it as similar to what my father taught me about the mind, which is that the mind is "tricky." As I aged, my meaning-making machine had fooled me into resistance in the form of meanings.

Some doctors and neuroscientists agree that the brain acts like a machine in the way it processes information, and mainly because it's always looking for meanings and comparing it only to the information that the brain already has. In essence, it's made to constantly make meanings regardless of what the meaning is. When I teach my clients, I like to call this meaning making machine "The Triple M." You make thousands of meanings a day unconsciously – based on many personal factors: the way you grew up, the culture and society you dwell in, your friends, social media, the news, your country, and your mental health. If you go to a movie exhausted, you might make the meaning that the movie was boring when really you were just tired. Or you might notice that a person you are talking to is giving you a nasty look when they simply have a piece of hair in their eye, and they are trying to blink. The Triple M is vast and tricky.

Like any machine, the Triple M has no attachment to the outcome of the meaning it sends out, just like the toaster (a machine) doesn't care if it burns the toast and the washing machine doesn't care if it ruins the clothes. It's just doing its best to make as many meanings as possible at lightning speed because *that's what it does.*

Resistance loves that we make meanings, because the dominant force of a meaning is to search for danger, keep us safe, and be accepted in our tribe (family, friends, and colleagues).

The machine is afraid of the unknown and uncertainty. Anything that is unknown or uncertain creates great resistance to moving forward. That's why we stay in comfort zones even when they are not healthy.

When you dive into writing you will notice all kinds of meanings your mind will make up to try to convince you that everything you write is terrible, or what you have to say doesn't matter, or a hundred other things. It might even make you afraid of success by making the meaning that success will be too much for you to handle. This is resistance doing its best work. As mentioned earlier, you never really know what you're going to write until you write it. But remember, resistance is hiding in the machine, and it is coded to stop us when we feel uncomfortable. It loves to warn you that what you're doing might offend, hurt, or bother someone, or worse – that people you love won't love you anymore.

The takeaway here? Don't believe your meanings. Start to question why and where those meanings come from.

For instance, Jenna was a very motivated student in my Create Your Dream Book program who was writing an amazing book on tarot in a way that has never been done. At the time, she was already an internationally-known tarot reader and entrepreneur based in the Pacific Northwest, with hundreds of testimonials. She knew she was good at what she does. Then one day her brother came to visit and said to her, "No one is ever going to read your book. There are too many books about tarot already."

Devastated and deflated, Jenna burst into tears when she recounted the story to my writing group; she also confessed that in the week since talking to her brother she hadn't written a word. Then one of the group members blurted out, "Does your brother even read books?"

That changed everything. Jenna paused for a moment, and laughed through her tears. "No," she said, "and he would never read a book about tarot. Why am I even letting this bother me?"

Then I jumped in. "Let's just say he did read books, or went to a bookstore – where would he look for a book he liked?"

Jenna wiped her eyes. "The mechanics or sport section!" We all laughed, and you could feel the relief ripple throughout the group. We could all identify with what Jenna was experiencing.

All it took was one person in her family to make one comment on something he knew nothing about to trigger her meaning-making machine. Her internal dialog went straight to worst case scenarios because her brain detected danger in the un-known, which was her book. Luckily, she was working with a writing group that had her back and she kept writing.

Questions / Thoughts for Inquiry

1. What is the meaning of life for you? Where did you get this meaning?

2. What meaning have you given yourself about being a writer?

3. Go to a mirror and say these words out loud three times while looking yourself in the eye. "I am a writer. This is the perfect time for me to write." I know that last one might sound hokey, but it's powerful medicine.

How to Crack a Code

Codes, also called ciphers (a secret or disguised way of writing or communicating) have been used for centuries to hide messages. Cryptanalysis is the word for "code-breaking," which involves studying codes with an eye toward discovering how they can be broken.

Here's an example of a code experienced by many writers: they obsess over ideas, sentences, dialog, scenes, and stories, and then freeze or avoid the writing process when they get close to starting or finishing it. More than anything, they want to know how to crack this code, break their resistance, and get their minds to focus on their writing, yet they remain stuck as if some kind of spell has taken over making them paralyzed or over-think everything.

Let's go back to code-breaking. To illustrate it I'll use an example commonly seen in movies: breaking into a safe. Consider a good cat burglar movie in which the burglar wants to steel a diamond necklace out of a well-guarded museum. Cat burglars are especially adept at entering and leaving the burglarized place without attracting notice. Let's pretend resistance has been living in the safe of your well-guarded mind for years. It's keeping you out of danger and wants nothing to do with taking risks.

This is how resistance works. It creeps into your mind and hijacks it, often without you realizing that it's there. Now let's pretend you are a cat burglar ready to crack the code, open the safe and destroy what's in it, so you can write freely whenever you want.

Think about what a cat burglar must do to successfully crack the code of a safe guarded by hundreds of cameras and tripwires and laser beams. First, they must study the architectural plans of the building, as well as information about where every guard is standing, when they switch shifts, and how the tripwires or lasers work. Next, they figure out what climbing gear they'll need to get to the top of the museum, and a way to lower themselves down just enough as to not touch the floor so they can reach the safe. Once they've cracked the code, they must get away without anyone noticing.

If this sounds impossible, it's not; in fact, it's been done by many thieves throughout history. It's admirable how cunning people can be when they really want something! I'm not advocating thievery, but I am suggesting that you apply the same concepts to facing your own resistance. The first is to agree that anything that gets in your way is, indeed, resistance. We call it doubt or fear. Others call it "hitting a wall." Whatever your challenges are, resistance is aware of them, because it has been taking notes since you were born, playing on your fears and guarding your greatest creative gifts. This means you've been living with the code you're about to crack for most of your life.

The good news is, it doesn't take a lifetime to crack it and create a new code or a new behavior. First, though, you must see it clearly. A good cryptanalyst can crack any security system if she knows its design and method of operation. The Greeks used the "Eureka" process, whereby they would find irregularities, mistakes or errors that helped crack the codes they were working on.

When you know how your mind works, you become your own cryptanalyst and can begin to crack the resistance code within. Remember, our minds get used to being a certain way. We get so used to our own habits that it can be hard to realize we are not living the life we were meant to live. We must begin the process of microscopic self-awareness, which in turn will help us use the "Eureka process." Once you find small irregularities in your thinking errors, you can crack your resistance code.

I discovered a sentence twenty years ago, written by Bill Harris, that I have repeated hundreds of times to my clients and at speaking events: "The mind cannot simultaneously be aware of an outmoded behavior and continue to do it."[1] Now you might be thinking, *"That's a load of crap because I'm aware I shouldn't eat chocolate cake and yet I still eat the cake.* However, if you look closely at that sentence, you'll see the secret. Most of the time we tell ourselves we want to do something differently but then we let one of our resistance styles step in and block our awareness. For instance, you may tell yourself that you're not going to eat cake after dinner, but then you fog up, or dissociate, or forget about your desire to act differently, and before you know it you've already eaten the cake. You didn't even stop to think about it. In this case there is no awareness. You were acting on autopilot.

What Harris is really saying is that you have to be extremely mindful – in other words, look for the pause and create awareness. Your mindfulness must include every aspect of the pattern, as if you were putting it under a microscope. If you were to observe yourself desiring the cake, then going to the cake and even cutting the cake, all the while thinking about

---

[1] Harris, Bill. (2007). *Thresholds of the Mind.* Centerpointe Press.

your promise to change that behavior, you might eat the cake once or twice, maybe three times, but your body and mind will react differently and you will stop doing it, if the desire to stop is genuine. You would simply begin to change your behavior because the mind would recognize that the cake no longer served you, and who wants to keep doing something that feels terrible over and over again? It's a natural process to stop because it will feel good to make a new decision and thus change the behavior.

The same is true for resistance as a writer. To break resistance, you have to get under the hood of your mind and figure out specifically what is going on in there, the same way that cat burglar has to investigate the code, lock or safe they want to crack open.

This is where curiosity becomes kryptonite for resistance.

Questions / Thoughts for Inquiry

1. Make an exhaustive list on the habits you do daily. (brush your teeth, make your bed, eat breakfast, work out, etc.)

2. Now that you know you are capable of training yourself to follow through, what writing habits would you like to create?

3. If you could easily create the habit to write daily or weekly, what would your ideal writing schedule look like? (it can be as little as 15 minutes a day, or as long as you think would be doable.)

Three Cs of Disaster: The Lion's Den of Resistance

With the internet and social media, we have access to millions of readers we never would have been able to reach in the past, which creates the potential for overnight success as well as overnight terror. Everything feels great when you first think about it... until you start thinking about what it means to be exposed to the masses. If you think too hard for too long about other people and other writers you will inevitably stumble into the lion's den of resistance, or what I call The Three Cs of disaster: Confusion, Comparison, and Catastrophe.

Confusion sets in almost immediately. We wonder whether we are writing it right, or in the right order, or if we are making any sense at all. You can always change lanes and change the course of your journey but the key is to have a basic map from the get-go so you get started – and stay on target.

Comparison is one of resistance's favorite treats. With 7.8 billion people in the world, it's easy to tell yourself that there are better writers than you. You could spend an entire month listing them, and in many cases you'd be right. However, you could also easily list tens of thousands of writers who are worse than you who made *The New York Times* Bestseller list. What you look for you will find. And remember that statistic I quoted earlier? Eight billion people in the world and even with so many people, there are still only about 600,000 new books coming out every year, which means there are way more content consumers than content creators. The world has an insatiable hunger for more content, and you can help fill that need!

I once asked a group of writers, "Do you think that there will be more weight loss books coming out?" When one woman blurted out, "Of course!" I then asked what the basic formula is to lose a pound. Though they described it in different ways, the consensus among the group was: "You have to put more energy out than you take in." Why, then, would anyone ever read another book on weight loss? It was obvious to them that we need new messengers to tell the same message for different people. A weight loss book written in 2022, though it might have the same basic formula, will be much different from one written in 1975. More important, these books are written from different perspectives, such as that of a college-age male or a woman in menopause. Know this: there is always an audience for a new perspective.

If you think your book is hitting a "flooded market," consider how many coffee shops are in your city? Hair salons? Car mechanics? The list goes on. There is really no such thing as a flooded market if you are passionate about the work you do or the books you write or the subjects you are writing about.

Remember, being yourself - staying true to your authenticity - will make you a champion writer. When people focus on doing what drives them, rather than trying hard to write about something you're not excited about, success comes naturally. Why? Because there is nothing more satisfying than creating something you're passionate about from scratch that has never been written by anyone but you.

Now let's talk about the third "C": catastrophic thinking. This is something my parents taught me a lot about, and they had plenty of material to use. Once upon a time, my father was an executive vice president in one of the most prestigious banks in Manhattan. He was a twenty-two-year veteran of the industry. He made it to Greenwich Savings Bank in Midtown Manhattan. He had a great pension, investments, my college fund, and all his ducks in a row... until the ducks collapsed during the savings bank crash of 1983, which put him out of work. Depression and alcohol took him down, and there was no more college fund. This created intense fights in the family due to confusion and sadness. In order to "save" me from ever getting my hopes up, he would always say, "You have to think of worst-case scenarios and be prepared for everything to go wrong." He figured if he gave me that bit of wisdom, I would be better off; instead, it had the opposite effect. I became terrified of "everything going wrong."

As writers we can torture ourselves, especially when we feel stress. This sets off alarms bells that can be very convincing for resistance but aren't actually happening in reality – they just feel like it because somewhere in our past either something went wrong, or our caregivers told us to watch out for the worst-case scenarios to keep us safe. Ninety-nine percent of the time there is nothing to fear, and the catastrophe never happens, yet the fear remains. The good news is, once we understand the origin of our personal fear, we are better able to dissolve resistance.

Questions / Thoughts for Inquiry

1. When was the last time you were confused about something and it worked out great? What did you do? How did you solve the confusion?

2. Who was the last person you compared yourself to as a writer? Is it possible that in the history of time someone less driven, and less smart than you wrote a book that was a best seller?

3. Make a list of three things you were super worried would happen but didn't. Take a deep look at the imaginary danger your brain created.

Ten Most Common

Resistance Styles

Whenever I see the bumper sticker that reads "No Fear," my first thought is, *Really? So, you're going to drive off a cliff?* We first need to realize fear is not inherently a bad thing – quite the opposite. It's a productive feeling and reaction that *prevents* us from jumping off that cliff. It's a warning that something might be dangerous. Interestingly, studies have shown that fear and excitement are linked, the only difference being how we breathe. Plus, it's a matter of perspective – for example, one person might be excited about a roller coaster ride, while another is petrified – and a discernment of risk, for example, when we do things we're afraid of, like getting married or skydiving it all depends on perspective. When true fear comes in we simply take the proper precautions, then take courageous action. Courage is simply acting in the face of fear. Everyone is courageous at some point in their life.

Resistance, on the other hand, rots our inner world. Resistance produces doubt, which is by far more dangerous than fear. It's a deceitful feeling, especially when it's obvious that our life is not on the line. Doubt creates inaction, resistance, and makes the smallest of actions feel like a death sentence.

Resistance is that invisible voice that tells you your writing sucks or reminds you of a time when you were teased at school. It's a feeling of utter paralysis, even when there is nothing in our way. It's a diabolical combination of doubt, dread and, sometimes, apathy. It also disguises itself as logical or "realistic" thinking when it is anything but. The key is to be able to identify your personal resistance style(s) so when they pop up you can say, "I see you, and I will not let you win." There are countless ways resistance can shapeshift, but after working with thousands of people and observing my own resistance for over a decade, I have found the following ten to be the most common.

1. Busyness/Impatience ("I have no time." or "This is taking too long.")

2. Fear of exposure ("If anyone sees this, they'll make fun of me.")

3. Procrastination (I'll do it later, first I have to do this other thing.")

4. Catastrophizing ("What if _____ happens?" (i.e., bad reviews, family hating you, people hating your work).

5. Comparing yourself to others ("I'll never be as good as _____ so why bother?"; "I'm too old/young.")

6. Boredom ("I'm not into my subject anymore, maybe it's not my thing.")

7. Perfectionism ("I have to reread it and rewrite over and over before I can show it to anyone or an editor"; "I suck!")

8. Disorganized + forgetful ("Oh, I meant to, but I forgot"; "I lost my file"; "I can't find it...I was just working on it!")

9. Freezing / Fogging up / Spacing Out ("I can't do this." or "What was I thinking?")

10. Addicted to overthinking ("I can't because I know there is an answer I have to think about.")

Symptoms of Resistance

The symptoms of resistance are endless and include anything that takes you away from your higher calling to create or write. Again, you must get microscopically clear on what your mind is telling you, or how you are feeling when you find yourself in resistance. Remember, if you wait until you feel like writing you will never write. You must learn to override the feeling of resistance, which become possible when we become aware of the styles that put us there.

Here are some examples of symptoms of resistance:

- Stagnation in life / unhealthy lifestyle / no movement

- Loss of enthusiasm / depression / shame/ guilt

- Hypersensitive/ anxiety / catastrophic thinking

- Tired / lonely /fatigued

- Addiction (i.e. drugs; alcohol; food; Netflix)

- Rationalization / justification/ perfectionism

- Victim stance (blaming external events or people)

- Perceived overwhelm/ problems with boundaries / lack of self-care

- Black-and-white thinking ("either-or" versus "both-and")

- No tolerance for adversity / cutting yourself off from others

Understanding Why We Drift Back into Resistance

If you've been in resistance for a long time, your mind and body will naturally want to revert back to their comfort zones. You might find yourself binging on Netflix, YouTube, social media, drinking, socializing and ignoring your writing or whatever form temptation takes for you. You must be keenly aware of the difference between taking a break and being knocked off your path by resistance, and you do this by accepting that EVERYTHING that gets in the way of your writing is resistance. Call it out, "I see you Mr. Resistance, and I know what you're up to. I am going to go back and finish my writing, so HA!"

Remember your thoughts are not to be trusted. Trust only your actions and, no matter what, get back to writing.

Questions / Thoughts for Inquiry

1. What is your number one resistance style?

2. What symptoms do you experience with this resistance style?

3. Are there more resistance styles that affect you? List your top three.

Resistance as a Shapeshifter

The most important thing to remember is that this ominous opponent, this thing called resistance, will morph into anything. Every thought we have is either a trick or a treasure, and the key is knowing the difference.

As mentioned earlier, I was sure when the pandemic struck that I would have the much- needed time to write all the things I'd been craving to write. I was so excited to be drowning in words... at first.

Then, as days and weeks went by, I noticed something that terrified me: despite the extra time, I was barely writing, (other than to jot down my immediate thoughts in my journal.) Resistance was following me like a lion who smelled the blood of its prey, and it came in many forms: covid fear and isolation, economic fear, political upheaval, burn-out, breakups, people dying, depression, binging on food, talking to friends and even walking in circles in my apartment. It seemed the whole world felt it too. I could feel a gigantic invisible cloud of global trauma take hold and create a forcefield of resistance. I kept hearing the small voice in my head saying, "Write!" – but nothing came out.

I was suffering in a way I had never imagined and, ironically, it was while I was working on this book! It was as if resistance had decided to go for the kill so I wouldn't expose it. My inner critic was so loud I spent one afternoon piling pillows on my head in an attempt to drown out the scowling faces of what resistance's shapeshifting was capable of. Suddenly imaginary faces of former professors, friends and family were judging me for being a coward. The clicking of my life clock was also especially loud. Tick. Tock. Tick. Tock. One minute I was too old, then I was still too young. Then I wasn't good enough. Then I was washed up but brilliant. I questioned my sanity.

Finally I decided to just be content and wait for inspiration to find me and here's the problem with that: people who decide to wait for inspiration to find them are dying a slow death. Waiting is not going to save you. What you fear you must dive into with action. Too much contentment can leave us rattled and often hating ourselves for wasting time. We saw this during covid. Millions went into quarantine and were suddenly faced with the scariest of realities: time. People saw that they could do the things they loved, and writers figured they would finally have their books written, and instead a massive wave of resistance hit the planet due to fear. Some seized the opportunity to create something new, while others fell into despair.

For resistance, this was its hay-day and it took full advantage of the tools at its disposal. More than ever, people were obsessed with their phones and social media in an attempt to stay "connected," even if it meant ignoring their dreams. Everyone was hanging over the dark cloud of uncertainty.

Uncertainty, doubt, and fear are not going anywhere anytime soon; they've been part of the human condition since the beginning of time. At some point we must accept it and embrace the freedom that comes from diving headlong into the fear of creativity. Ninety-nine percent of the time the fear is imaginary. If you want to disarm resistance, hold your finger to your closed lips and audibly make the sound "shhhhhhhh." You have to make resistance know you are aware of it.

Questions / Thoughts for Inquiry

1. Practice sitting in silence for five minutes a day. No more, no less. Listen for neutral sounds like a fan, or cars driving by. Just listen. If you have a thought, go back to listening for a sound, even if it's the sound of silence.

2. Do you usually find yourself thinking about the past or the future? When you feel stress (or resistance) jot down which way your minds goes? Is it a past thought triggering the stress or a future thought?

3. Anytime during the day, take two minutes to write your worry thoughts down on paper with a pen. Don't judge it. Just let it flow and walk away.

PART II

Know Yourself

Learn Your Dominant
F3 Response

The fight, flight, or freeze response (referred to as "F3" by the military) is the body's system for responding to threats, real or perceived. As mentioned earlier, this system is located in the most primitive – or reptilian – part of the brain at the base of our skull. Psychology has recently added a fourth response called "fawn" but we are going to stick to the traditional three as it relates to our physiology. These particular F3 responses are involuntary in our biology and sets off a number of physiological changes that help someone:

- fight, or take action to eliminate the danger

- flee, which involves escaping the danger

- freeze, which involves becoming immobile

The term "fight or flight" dates back to the 1920s, when psychologist Walter Bradford Cannon coined it to describe this neurochemical "discharge." When we encounter a sudden threat, our adrenals pump out hormones that trigger various glands to flood our bloodstream with epinephrine, better known as adrenaline, along with a potent cocktail of norepinephrine, estrogen, testosterone, cortisol, dopamine, and serotonin. Our heartbeat and breath quicken. Our pupils dilate. Our stomachs clench. Embarrassingly, our sexual organs may wake up. In a flash, we're ready for survival – primed with greater strength, heightened awareness, and quicker reaction time.

Therefore, when you hear the words, "Look out!" you move faster than you would have believed possible to escape an assailant or get out of the path of the rock about to fall on your head.

We all have a dominant F3 response, and once you understand yours you will know another way resistance sneaks up on you when you sit down to write. Oftentimes, this can be traced back to your childhood – for instance, if you were abused, bullied, and/or living in fear, these experiences would have shaped your response. We learn at a young age which of the responses – fight, flight or freeze – works best.

Remember how much my father taught me to protect myself from danger at all costs? Well, my cousin, an NYPD officer, instructed me to avoid anything that even looked dangerous. "If the cops are running in one direction," he'd often say, "you run the other way, got it?"

My dad also taught me to read the energy of people when I rode the subways. He said, "If something ever feels off, and you'll feel it in your gut, trust yourself. Get off that subway car and find one with the conductor or take a different train." This also applied when I was walking down dark streets or approached by strangers. The rule was, "Don't worry about embarrassing yourself or your friend's making fun of you; if something doesn't feel right, get out of there."

There were many times I walked off a train and waited for the next one, only to find out later that a gun had been fired or someone pulled a knife. Sometimes I walked twelve blocks out of my way to get home because something either looked or felt suspicious on a particular block, or it was too dark.

The second thing Dad and my peers taught me was how to fight, but only if I had to protect myself. I would practice self-defense with my father when I was sixteen and he showed me various places to grab or kick an attacker so I had time to get away. I was also taught that if all else fails to remain very calm and still and assess the situation and "act dumb" until I could figure out what to do.

As you can see, "flight" became my number one dominant F3 response and "fight" was number two.

A Writer in Flight

Given these experiences, I can see why I seem to wind up in a different room as soon as I sit down to write. It's as if I'm in some magic show – the laptop suddenly turns into the kitchen counter and I'll be making tea and thinking, *How did I get in here?* This happens so often I must find ways to stay seated. (Note: I'm not ADD or ADHD) It is my flight response kicking in because my mind perceived entering into the unknown journey of creativity as dangerous.

Does this sound familiar? If so, and you find yourself engaged in some form of procrastination instead of writing, it could be that your dominant F3 response is flight. When you experience mental agitation, you will seize any opportunity to escape rather than face it.

A Writer in Fight

If you are prone to fighting when you're in danger this is the response that will kick in when entering the unknown presents itself as a threat. You want to write, but your words seem stiff and unyielding and it's hard to get them on paper. This feeling of being locked up or caged typically triggers your primal fight instinct. Perhaps you feel as if you must sit there and suffer, so you beat yourself mentally. For example, you might circle back to the same sentence twenty times berating yourself for the terrible job you're doing. This leads you down memory lane of how you're a good-for-nothing piece of poo and certainly nowhere as good of a writer as others. You may then turn to things to numb your mental anguish through alcohol, TV, or whatever else "turns off" your brain.

A Writer in Freeze

When someone is in the freeze response they basically are in suspension in place. Among writers, the most common example of this is staring at a blank page and feeling like a failure.

Each of these response styles is useful in certain real-life dangerous situations, but they are not very conducive to writing. By their very design, they're stronger than anything else going on at the moment, which means that when they kick in they grab all of your attention and you end up focusing on the triggering issue instead of your writing.

The bottom line is that F3 responses are natural and here to stay – the question is how they show up in your writing life. Once you start building your awareness around these mental triggers, you'll be able to overcome any fear-based resistance, rather than being a victim for why you're not making progress with your work.

How do you build this awareness? It's a matter of practice and finding ways to train your mindset to not allow an F3 response to take over. That's why writing in small bursts is helpful.

Try setting your alarm for a short time, which will relieve some of the pressure and make it more likely that you not only can identify it, but you will conquer it. Then, gradually increase the length of time, building your confidence step by step. These small wins bring big rewards as you train yourself to stay relaxed and calm when you write.

Questions / Thoughts for Inquiry

1. What do you think your dominant F3 response is as a writer?

2. The next time you sit down to write become aware of your F3 response. To test it out, set a timer for five minutes and try not to stop writing, see if your F3 response emerges.

3. If you experience all three, in what order do you experience them?

Your Origin of Fear Story

Can you find a time in your childhood when you were scared and were either taught or figured out how to avoid/escape danger? It could be something you learned at home or in school.

After being accepted to Eastern Washington University's MFA in Creative Writing program, I needed to establish residency so I could afford to attend, which meant I had to live in Washington state for one year to get the residency tuition which was much less than an out of state student. During that year I noticed something odd. Whenever I tried to sit down and write I would have a panic attack or get anxiety. My F3 responses were bouncing off walls, but I was too young to know what was causing it. There I was, about to begin one of the most competitive MFA programs in the nation and I couldn't write! I felt like the biggest imposter.

In graduate school each of us had been assigned counselor-coaches who would help us navigate the writing program. I decided to book an appointment with mine before classes started. John Keeble was a *Washington Post* writer and a *New York Times* bestselling author. I remember feeling so intimidated as I walked into the downtown Spokane school building. He was straight forward and asked me how I was doing. I assumed that meant in my writing. I could feel my voice shaking as I confessed that for the last year, I hadn't written anything as I admitted every time I tried to write I got so anxious I would cry and felt like a total failure.

"I must not be a writer after all," expecting my soon-to-be professor to suggest I pack it up and go back home to New York City.

Instead, he stunned me by asking, "Do you think like a writer?"

I nodded.

"Do you see the world like a writer? Do you eavesdrop and think certain conversations would make great dialog?"

I nodded.

"Then you're simply a writer who is not writing and your job is to find out why. Investigate that," he said.

He made it seem like the most natural thing in the world. I have never forgotten his words. Sure enough I started writing when I had the support of a group and a mentor.

If you can answer yes to the question, "Do you think like a writer?" and you know in your heart that you want to write, then you are a writer! As you build on your self-awareness, and learn strategies to kick resistance to the curb, you will realize, and own the fact that you are *always* a writer, even when you're not writing.

Think about the origin of your own fear story. While we don't want to get stuck in the past, investigating it informs our future and is liberating – especially when it leads to the resolution of resistance crisis that you are facing.

Questions / Thoughts for Inquiry

1. Where do you think you learned your F3 response to danger? It probably happened when you were young.

2. What is the bravest thing you've ever done?

3. Practice simply thinking like a writer. What ideas have you thought of recently? Jot down ideas, dialogue ideas, title ideas and have fun with it.

The Loop of Doom

(and how to jump out of it)

Plot twist: our brains have not caught up with evolution. In most parts of the world, we are safer than we've ever been, yet we suffer from more anxiety than at any other time in history. Our minds continue to mess with us, always perceiving the unknown as a threat. This is why when you finally sit down to write (unless you have created a consistent habit of doing so) the loop of doom sets in. I define the loop of doom as those what-ifs (what if...my writing sucks; people don't like it, and so on) that send us running back to our F3 response and comfort zones of inaction. Some call this "the drift," in which we unconsciously drift back into whatever takes us away from writing because we fear the discomfort of the blank page.

People are desperate to feel safe, calm, and stress free. The problem is that much of our anxiety around our writing is a figment of our imagination that no pill, or book, or therapist can get rid of. Many times we don't want to even admit our fears to ourselves, let alone our therapists or coaches, because it sounds so silly; for example: "I think my writing is going to cause a complete mental breakdown," or "I'm afraid that my mother's sister's neighbor will read my book and think it's about her and my entire support network will crumble" or "What if I get on a celebrity talk show and have to explain what I was writing about?" or "What if after I put all that effort into my book, no one reads it?" (Which, by the way, is impossible in the twenty-first century. You will always have readers.) Resistance will scare you into thinking all sorts of crazy things just to keep you safe and send you back into the loop of doom where you feel terribly unsatisfied, and yet crave the comfort. It's the place in which you tell yourself that maybe tomorrow you will feel better. Tomorrow you will write. Then tomorrow comes and you are back in the loop.

Here's the rub: once we loop back into our comfort zone, we get a different kind of anxiety. As the days go by and we are not writing, we begin to feel resentful, bitter, and trapped. It's the feeling that our lives are passing us by and we're not stepping into our soul's calling. The words and stories in our heads and hearts are stuck again. We even draw comfort by telling ourselves lies like maybe we are not writers after all or now is just not the right time to write. It is in these moments that the loop of doom and resistance give each other a big high five!

Resistance whispers, "Honey, I'm on your side. Remember, I want you to be safe and if it doesn't feel good to write, you shouldn't. There's no reason to put yourself through torture… after all, if it doesn't give you immediate gratification it's not worth it, right?"

Don't Believe Your Thoughts

When I first read the phrase "Don't believe your thoughts" found in so many self-help books, I was like, "*You have to be kidding me. My thoughts are like gorillas pounding and bouncing off the walls of my brain. If I try to ignore them they pound their chests more until I submit!*"

Then I learned that the proper way to manage my mind was *not* by trying to ignore my thoughts, but by accepting that they are part of the meaning making-machine and not taking them so seriously. The best part of cracking your resistance code is learning to stay neutral no matter what you're thinking. You want to learn to say to yourself, "It's just a thought" whenever you feel resistance. It's like mothering your inner child and letting that child know that you've got things under control and you are not being chased by predators, you're just writing. You must teach your gorillas to trust you.

Consider this: we think about eighty-five thousand thoughts a day, and ninety percent of them are the same day after day. This means unless we learn how to throw a monkey wrench into the machine of our thoughts, we are going to wake up thinking the things we thought when we went to sleep the night before. If you're like most of the world, those thoughts are dominated by your problems, and if so that's the loop of doom at its best.

We crack the resistance code in ourselves by first understanding how to stop the loop of doom. It starts with awareness. You will not escape the loop of doom unless you are first willing to watch it play out.

There are three ways to navigate this.

1) **"Trust Yourself."** Like most cliches, this one holds an essential truth that is often forgotten or dismissed. For our purposes, trusting yourself means understanding what makes you tick by watching your behavior closely.

2) **There is Nothing Wrong with You.** Things just take

practice. I know this is a hard one. Just as the acorn has everything it needs to become the oak tree; you have everything you need to be the writer you've always wanted to be. This is true for any endeavor, be it golfing, painting, or learning how to fly a plane. Sure, you will need to learn some skills and techniques, but you first have to embrace the above truth.

3) **Your Belief Systems are Not Your Fault.** On one hand you need to take responsibility for your behaviors and actions, but what you believe about yourself is not your doing, but the result of possible bad parenting, societal norms, or surrounding yourself by people who hold you back. The good news is, you can undo old belief systems and replace them with new ones. You get to start right from where you are and learn how to be unstoppable and enjoy life as a writer in a way you never thought possible. When I say, "Your belief systems are not your fault," I'm asking you to consider how you've been hypnotized into thinking you are a particular "type" of person and therefore you act a certain way. Resistance loves types. It loves to convince you that you are too small, too tall, too this or that. For decades resistance and fear have been telling you lies based, not only on your real-life events, but those of others who pass their stories onto you. Until now. From here on out, you are free to be the real you.

Questions / Thoughts for Inquiry

1. What negative beliefs do you have about yourself as a writer?

2. Are these beliefs 100% true all the time?

3. Is it possible the opposite belief is actually truer?

Decision Fatigue
vs. Willpower

Another way to crack your resistance code and train your brain is to prepare for "decision fatigue."

What Is Decision Fatigue?

Studies have shown we have a certain amount of brain energy to make decisions. When we make too many at once it affects our ability to choose what's best for ourselves. This starts when you first wake up. It could be a small decision like looking at a text message, which leads to a meme or to a link, which then leads to a social media account, which then leads to watching or clicking the news or more social media accounts. It could be a big decision like buying a car, or getting a loan, or a job application. Either way we use up a certain amount of mental energy.

Perhaps the most compelling study found was that judges were significantly more likely to grant parole in the morning than afternoon. Morning cases were released seventy percent of the time, while those in the late afternoon saw a release rate of less than ten percent – even when the facts of those cases were similar! Other studies confirmed the existence of decision fatigue and that we often "wasted" our decision-making capability on small things like checking our phones in the morning and debating which meme to send to our friends.

Not too long ago, the prevailing belief was that we get through anything if we were willing to "tough it out." Now we know that using "willpower" is often not sustainable in the long-term. This is especially true with creative endeavors, yet writers continue to feel like they are failing when they are out of mental energy.

The Problem with Willpower

Psychological tests have proven that willpower is not, as the name suggests, an endless stream of power that we can summon at will. It is a limited resource, and the more you use on making unimportant decisions, the more open you are to temptations and distractions that knock you off your goals.

Resistance loves it when our willpower runs dry and it especially loves that we think we can conquer resistance with willpower alone. Trust me, I've imagined how resistance rubs its hands together with a bloodcurdling laugh whenever a writer says, "I will use my willpower to beat my resistance!"

What we judge as being "not interested" in our writing, or thinking we are writing the "wrong" book, could actually be plain old decision fatigue. We might be blowing off our writing, thinking, *I guess I'm not a writer after all,* when really, it's a situational problem because you had a difficult day, didn't create the proper priorities, or used up your decision-making capabilities and become too mentally exhausted to follow through with your dream book or writing project.

When you become decision fatigued, you're more likely to return to the loop of doom a.k.a comfort zones that make you blank out.

Here's a scenario that might sound familiar. You use your phone as an alarm clock and when it goes off you make the decision to hit snooze. Instead you check to see if your post from last night got a few likes. Then you see you have four new text messages, three Facebook messages, and a voicemail. You've got emails too – some personal, some work-related and before you know it, your mind is scrambling to address them, but you also have to pee. What to do first? You get to the bathroom and remember you have to get ready for work. Do you have meetings? Do you need to put on pants, or can you get away with just a hoodie? It's a Zoom meeting, you need to look up the link. Do you need makeup? Can you get away with just lipstick? Do you need pants? Will pajama bottoms be okay? What are you going to eat for breakfast?

You remember you had planned a five-minute meditation and write for at least fifteen minutes each morning, but now you're telling yourself that can wait until later. You throw a few things in the laundry and the machine starts to make a funny noise – something else you have to deal with. One hour (or more) into your day you might have made over a hundred decisions without even noticing. Ba-bye willpower, that muscle doesn't have a chance.

Looking at this scenario, it's easy to see why Benjamin Franklin had it right when he said, "If you fail to plan, you plan to fail." This has never been truer than in the twenty-first century, where distractions are literally the play game of the day.

Let's re-examine the same scenario, this time with your new mind training and strategy in place.

A lot of successful artists, entrepreneurs, creatives, and inventors opt to create certain routines when they embark on a project. The idea is that when you have a safe container, as in a routine that is simple and predictable, you will have more energy, mental clarity, and freedom. For instance, let's say you have planned out your meals and what you'll wear that week. You also use a regular alarm clock, keeping it far enough away that you have to get up; your smartphone is not within arm's reach, and you have the notifications (including those for social media platforms) turned off. You get up, set the timer for your five-minute meditation, then walk over to your writing area and write for fifteen or twenty minutes. The less time you spend on decisions that are not adding to your writing goals, the more time you have for writing and creating something you're proud of.

Questions / Thoughts for Inquiry

1. Don't check your smart phone or pick up your computer, iPad, tablet for 30 minutes upon waking tomorrow and feel the difference in your day.

2. Plan on writing for 15-30 minutes tomorrow.

3. Tell everyone who might get in your way that you are 100% NOT available during that time, unless someone is bleeding or it's a legitimate emergency.

NOTE: if someone or something does get in your way and you didn't write, write about what got in your way and how you will prepare better for the next day.

The Big O

Overwhelm. I hear this word over and over, literally hundreds of times, from clients, students, and my audience. Resistance loves overwhelm because nothing is more efficient at stopping us in our tracks than the concept of overwhelm.

Let's dissect this for a moment now that we understand decision fatigue, willpower, and how easy it is to buy into our meaning-making thoughts. In my experience, no writer can avoid the feeling of overwhelm. Why? Because there will be a point in virtually every writing project when you will feel you've bitten off more than you can chew. In fact, I believe it is a rite of passage for writers to fully embody overwhelm and learn how to dissolve it. The secret of conquering the "Big O" is to do the opposite of what we usually want to do: we need to slow down. Slowing down feels so strange when you are overwhelmed and yet it's the only way to defeat it. Learn to do things one step at a time. You'll soon realize that if you are able to stay in the present moment, overwhelm disappears.

One of my former coaches said that overwhelm happens when you are afraid of becoming intimate with the present moment and instead dwell too much on a future that doesn't yet exist or a past that is gone. It's when you are obsessing about all the things that have gone wrong or could go wrong in your world. It's also a paralysis that stems from the feeling that you're behind in life and need to speed things up. In every case, you have lost sight of the power and potentiality of the present moment.

Your internal dialog might sound like this: "Oh my God, what have I gotten myself into? I can't do this. Who am I to write about anything? It's all been done before, who wants to read another memoir/ business or productivity guide/ mommy blog/ story of overcoming challenges, fiction story about a mystery, etc . . .? Plus, my car needs new brakes, and I have to get back into shape. Maybe I should just start exercising and put this off. I can't do this right now. What if it doesn't get published? What if it *does* get published? What if I miss out on things because I'm spending all my time writing? What will I miss out on if I don't get this writing done?"

That's when you stop.

Breathe.

The truth is you are not alone in your thoughts. We've all been paralyzed by doubt at some point.

The easiest and best way to counter the feeling of overwhelm is to breathe slowly, do a body scan to relax your body, and embrace the moment at hand.

I love this quote from Bill Murray. He said:

> *"The more relaxed you are, the better you are at everything: the better you are with your loved ones, the better you are with your enemies, the better you are at your job, the better you are with yourself... It's incredibly important to be relaxed – you don't have a chance if you're not relaxed. So I try very hard to relax any kind of tension."*

When overwhelm hits, you must do the counterintuitive thing and stop thinking about the past and the future and decide that just for a few minutes you will honor yourself and get as intimate with the moment as possible. Some call this mindfulness – a word I think is overused and misunderstood. That said, for me mindfulness has always implied getting better at one thing at a time and stop trying to fix anything. You're not trying to be a better person. You are simply desiring to connect to the moment – to the air flowing in and around you, to your beating heart, to the muse that will arrive now that you're creating space for her to help you write. It is connection to your true self.

Mindfulness and a deep sense of relaxation is the greatest gift you can give yourself before any act of creation. It is a powerful tool for anyone who wants to improve their life in any way. It's not just about reducing stress or achieving spiritual fulfillment, but rather creating the foundation needed so that we can stay focused on what matters most to us: enjoying the process! It is about creating an environment where resistance cannot survive.

Questions / Thoughts for Inquiry

1. If you experience a feeling of overwhelm when you write what do you think is causing it? Are you thinking too much about what will happen after you write, do you feel like everything you're writing about sucks? It's important to understand where your mind goes when you get stuck in the big O.

2. Are you afraid of failure or are you afraid of success? Does your mind tell you to fear that your book will flop or that your book could be wildly successful and then you'll be seen by thousands?

3. Write two columns. In column one write down all the things you're afraid of in your book is a "failure" in your eyes. In column two write down what you're afraid of if your book is wildly successful. Which column is longer?

Sitting Down to Write

After enduring two years of quarantine, and having studied everything I could get my hands on about how resistance is coded into our minds, I still found myself fighting the silence, and experiencing resistance. Finally, I decided to call in one of my best friends to write with me. All I needed was for someone, preferably a writer and friend, to sit in the room with me while I was writing.

Liz, a good friend, and fellow writer, was the perfect choice. I loved the way she seemed to drop into flow easily. Liz was emotionally stronger than me, precise and dedicated in a way I admired. I was still fragile from the difficult year in quarantine, and it had become a terror to be alone with myself and stare at a blank page.

I called Liz and asked if she would come over to my place to work for a few hours so I could finally get in the flow. "Sure. I'll bring tea," she said.

Thirty minutes later she walked into my home and gave me a big hug. Hugs meant more to me now with the whole "social distancing." Covid had created a new "touchless normal" that first year of the pandemic and, since I was single, I hadn't realized how much I relied on that touch to keep me sane.

"Just grab any seat," I told her. "Dining room table. Use my desk or the couch, whatever's clever for you." Liz had been over before but usually we were watching movies or talking about men.

Liz came from a pretty crazy family herself, yet she knew a secret that I was just beginning to understand. She knew that following her calling as a writer was a way to show herself love, and it grounded her. She would not let resistance or fear overcome her deep desire to be what she was meant to be. Liz, who's a few years older, made it very clear that she had also gone through a lot of trauma before finding peace in her writing. Her secret: she didn't write alone. She had a small handful of writers with whom she always stayed connected and that helped her write almost every day. I realized I needed that.

Within three minutes Liz was already sitting at the far-right end of the dining room table with a cup of green tea. I walked to the left end of the table and opened my laptop. She was wearing all white. She wore white a lot. I wondered if wearing white made a person more focused. We had been friends for a decade and all of a sudden, I couldn't stop staring at her graceful concentration and wondering if wearing white was her secret. Part of me wanted to pour a glass of red wine on her just to mess up her perfect white sweater and pants.

"Why all the white?" I asked.

"It's my way of reminding myself to enjoy the moment. I buy all my white clothes on sale because they get dirty fast and I have to throw them away."

I couldn't help noticing the contrast between us – I was wearing black boots, black jeans and a black t-shirt.

Liz and I looked like a yin-yang.

"Alexa, play Vivaldi," I said.

Liz's posture was perfect. She was as fanatical about yoga as she was about writing. Those two things ruled her life. I promised internally to start doing yoga the next day. Would that help my writing? I was in awe of how Liz never lifted her head from her screen and was still typing. I finally started to write and noticed twenty-five minutes had gone by.

I had gone from avoiding writing to judging myself harshly. I was scared and afraid I would never be like Liz. I started thinking about how my writing would never amount to anything. Thoughts of old age came rushing in. Perhaps I'm too old for writing. Maybe I am worn out. Maybe I'll never amount to anything. Then I remembered. I was having F3 responses, and my resistance styles were taking over. There was nothing wrong, I was falling into the trap that resistance loves. The fear of the unknown. Confusion, comparison, and catastrophe.

"You are not going to win, "I whispered secretly and started pounding the keyboard like my life depended on it, which it did.

Finally, I was writing.

Questions / Thoughts for Inquiry

1. Do you have a favorite place to write? At home, in a coffee shop with a friend?

2. Make a short quick list of people who you can call if you get stuck in resistance.

3. Try new environments to write in. Go someplace you are not familiar with, like a library or write with a friend.

PART III

Know Divine Forces

You Were Born for This

There are forces and divine energy waiting for you to finally embrace your calling as a writer. Whenever we make a solid choice to create a life we love and follow a dream, there is one force much greater than any resistance you will ever experience, and that force is everywhere just waiting for you to commit. I call that force God. Some call it the Divine, others might call it Fran. I'm going with the word God. God is not responsible for you and that is why we have free will. You are responsible for you. However, once you ask for help and commit to your dream, so many things will line up for you that you will start to believe in miracles. Carl Jung called this the super conscious. What I know is that once you tap into it, all sorts of things start to fit into place. You must learn to trust this energy and you must learn to leap in order to know that a net will catch you.

The Three C's to Break Through Resistance

Talent is only ten percent of the equation Action, determination and follow-through are ninety percent of what makes success happen. There is only one thing that is required of you to tap into this endless divine energy that will guide you and drive you to the finish line: one hundred percent commitment. Commitment at this level kills resistance.

Once that commitment is made, seemingly out of nowhere everything starts to fit into place and the resistance takes a back seat. It's a phenomenon written about since the beginning of time.

I created a very simple system that allows you to cultivate inspiration, call in your muse, and gather the forces around you to make the process seamless and easy. It's called, "My Three C's Break Through Resistance System: Courage, Consistency and Compassion." That last one, compassion, is something we all forget and it's what sets us back the most. We must learn to be compassionate towards ourselves.

Courage

It takes courage to show up. It doesn't mean we aren't scared; it means we take action despite the fear. An easy way for you to tap into your courage is to remember that God would not have given you the desire to write if you were not meant to do it. Think about it. Do you walk around wishing you were an architect or a mechanic or a doctor? Probably not. Your job is to just keep moving forward one step at a time, one word at a time. We are all powerful creators, and if you're willing to take action and you refuse to quit, you literally cannot fail.

Consistency

Remember, great writers don't start out great and many "talented" writers never get started because they can't sit down and commit. Just as surely as a musician practices his instrument or an athlete practices to get better at a sport, you must be consistent in your writing practice. You must trust the process of taking action daily (or at least weekly) so that you build your writing muscles and discover the magic within your words. Again, the key is to be messy about it. Don't ever try to write anything perfectly on the first go or you'll be staring at the same sentence for days without really getting to the heart of your own voice and style.

Compassion

You're going to slip up. You're going to have a bad day, or forget to write, and this is when the third C of compassion is the most important. You must have compassion for yourself. Perfection is not the goal. The goal is progress. You can't beat yourself up for not writing or think you're a bad person or a bad writer. Gratitude or appreciation is always an excellent antidote. Be grateful for who you are, your tenacity and your ability to follow your dream. Look around your room or home and all the beautiful things God has gifted you with. Come back to the present moment and relax. Keep coming back to the writing with an open heart and you will naturally find yourself doing the work with courage and consistency.

If you are willing to be in gratitude and be patient with yourself while you are being consistent you will create a huge shift in your perspective and your behavior. You will become a magnet for the forces of energy that will guide you forward.

I consider compassion to be one of the most important parts of getting past creative resistance, because it allows you to organically bust through it and come out the other side a new person. Your compassion for yourself will bring you joy, and that new energy will feed your writing with more inspiration. You will also find yourself inspiring others with your newfound joy.

I'd like to share the story of a woman (we'll call her Veronica) who reached out to ask about my writing coaching services. Veronica said she was a very spiritual woman who connected deeply with the divine and had a magical story to tell about her life. She wanted to help the world with her inspiring story because she was turning forty-nine and didn't want to turn fifty without the book being written. Veronica had the whole thing drafted in her head, and it was a magnificent book idea that deserved to be shared. The story would benefit many people since it was about how she overcame big struggles to live a gifted life. She asked about my process as a coach, specifically how I structured my one-on-ones and how I inspired people to write and find their muse. I explained that being inspired to write is often a temporary feeling unless you have a plan to stay consistent. "The muse will meet you at your writing desk," I said, "once she knows where to find you." I went on to say that inspiration is not something you wait for, but rather something you create and develop, from the inside out. That's when she cut me off.

"Oh no," she said. "It will pour out of me perfectly when I am ready. I just have to wait until I feel like doing it."

I sighed knowing that she was in resistance. Last I checked she still hasn't written the book.

Beware of these dangerous words:

"I just have to wait until I feel like doing it."

You will rarely, if ever, 'feel like doing it'. It breaks my heart when I hear how people think the writing process should be "inspired", and that they dream of being saved by inspiration, which is just that, a dream. Waiting for inspiration is a backward formula. Taking action creates inspiration.

Questions / Thoughts for Inquiry

1. Ask yourself, "Who do you have to become to be consistent?" It's best to not think of consistency as "forever" or our human brain might immediately rebel. Even for the most disciplined, "forever" is a tall order, and many of us don't even like the word discipline, even if it's something that is good for us.

2. What is your writing plan? Let's say you want to write 20,000 words, and you want to get it done in ninety days. At this point you need to "reverse engineer" the project by coming up with a daily or weekly word count so you can stay on track.

3. Ask yourself: What might I have to give up temporarily or shift in order to hit my goal?" For instance, perhaps you can wake up a half-hour earlier each day, or create solid boundaries in the evenings so you have the quiet time to write.

Myth of Solitude

I meet so many people who get stuck for the simple reason that they are trying to do something alone (this includes writing a book.) If God wanted us to go it alone in life, He would have given each of us our own planet and left us to fend for ourselves. One of the greatest gifts we have is the ability to connect to divine energy that is guiding us every step of the way. We are also here to be of support to likeminded souls. There is no need to make writing a lonely endeavor, and many great writers had groups, large or small, they relied on to help them keep going.

There is a long-standing myth of the noble writer who slaves away in solitude and – voila! walks out of their house with a bestseller in hand. Anyone who has read Henry David Thoreau's *Walden Pond* has romanticized the idea of a writer going into the woods and writing a masterpiece all by themselves. The irony is that Thoreau lived one mile from Walden Pond and didn't isolate himself to write. He would write a few hours in the day and then go home where his mother and sister would do his laundry, feed him, and give him feedback on his work!

Hemingway moved to France and found a very tight-knit group of writers who helped each other write and thrive. And the list goes on. Author Liz Gilbert had a writing group, and Brené Brown didn't think she could write until she created a small group to allow her to speak her books out loud into a recording device and … the rest is bestselling history.

We also somehow got it in our heads that every bestselling book was a masterpiece from the first draft. What most people forget, or don't realize, is that every book, every essay, every blog, and every poem is usually written like messy at first, just to get the basic idea out and to see where the story or idea is going.

This is why tapping into the divine and creating community are so important. When you find someone to help you or write with you, you will be that much more successful in creating the book of your dreams. You do have to be careful to choose people who are one hundred percent on board with your vision, but it's worth it. You cannot fail if you do not quit, and it's harder to quit when your friends, coach, or writing group has your back. I often ask myself who the best person would be to read my drafts, and if I can't find a good group or the right person, I hire a writing coach. The bottom line is that the easiest and best way to get a book finished and out into the world is to have a small team of like-minded souls to help you.

Questions / Thoughts for Inquiry

1. Who are you surrounding yourself with? Are they cheering you on?

2. Do you know any other writers that might want to be your accountability partner?

3. Look for groups in your city or online. You want to be in an environment that nurtures who you really are, and what you're capable of, and at least one person who will lift you up when you are feeling down about your writing.

Embracing Uncertainty

Life and writing have much in common. You just don't know what will happen next. You think you know what your book is going to be about, then suddenly you're writing something unexpected that you never would have thought of had you not been writing. When you embark on the journey to write you are entering into chaos, but this chaos will eventually form order. I like to think of it as entering the eye of the storm. You watch the chaos around you as you stay calm and enjoy it. Once you accept the uncertainty of it all you can embrace the present moment. You realize it's not actually about "getting there" but rather about being curious and enjoying the process of discovery. We often assume that when we are stuck with an idea, the harder we think about it the closer we will get to finding the answer... until we remember that our mind is just a tool, not the key to salvation. You are not your mind. You are not what you think. You are not even what you do. You are a human *being*. Thoughts are being thought *through* you. You are a conduit to get the message out to the world via your writing. This requires you to trust yourself, your angels and your guides.

I believe that God and all divine energy is able to communicate with us when we learn to calm our mind and go into a place of stillness. This can happen when we are walking our dog, on a hike, driving, sitting in silence, or having fun. Many of the greatest inventions and discoveries were done when the person least expected it. As Eckhart Tolle wrote in *The Power of Now*, "All true artists, whether they know it or not, create from a place of no-mind, from inner stillness. Even the great scientists have reported that their creative breakthroughs came at a time of mental quietude."

The words for your story or book must travel from your mind (thoughts), through your body, and then to the page – and that's a long way to go! It is hard to capture what we really want to say or convey, and as odd as it may seem, the logical mind is not always the best ally to get us there. It's important to feel your way through your writing in order to take your audience on the journey with you.

Our conscious mind can only pay attention to a limited amount of stuff at one time, and when we get stressed it gets even more limited. This is why we have to trust the process and know that it's not just our conscious mind writing, but also our subconscious mind. When we are stuck the best thing to remember is that resistance is always temporary.

When we repeatedly play sports or a musical instrument, the subconscious mind keeps working on muscle memory to improve performance. The same is true for writing – even when you're doing something else, the mind continues to work out the kinks so that when you come back to your computer or paper you discover new avenues and solutions to your work that eluded you the day or week before.

Here's an analogy I love to share with clients or students who are afraid of the unknown territory of writing. "Imagine if I brought you to a gorgeous piece of land that spanned fifty acres and had a stream on it. You will be provided with food and shelter and you won't get hurt. The catch is that I have buried a hundred highly valuable gold nuggets, worth ten thousand dollars each, in the dirt and in the stream. I give you a sifter and tell you that it might takes hours or weeks, but as long as you continue to search you will not fail to find gold." Odds are you would be elated and think, *Yeah! I'm going to sift and be rich!* You would grab the tools and start digging. It would be uncomfortable - you'd get tired and probably consider quitting or think I was lying – but my guarantee that you will find the gold keeps you going. Low and behold, after a few days of digging and sifting you have found fifty gold nuggets! No doubt you were motivated to keep going long before that – from the time you found the very first nugget.

That's what it feels like to write. You have to trust the process and dig and dig and dig; if you do, if you keep coming back to the page, I guarantee that you will always find those hidden gems. You will get better and better and eventually feel more comfortable with uncertainty, and that is the key.

The Unknown is where all possibility lives. The known is just a stagnant place of complacency. The illusion that inaction is a safe place to be is one of the greatest weapons of resistance. Complacency is just another word for resistance. Creative energy is uncomfortable, but when you know the universe has your back, you start to enjoy the discovery process.

Action Steps

It's time to write your sloppy first copy of a chapter. It can be as little as a page or as long as you like, but first follow these simple steps:

1. **Brain dump every idea you have for your book or story.** I mean everything, emails you might have written, ideas you've jotted down, anything you can think of that you want to include in your book, be it a short book or long book.

2. **Then mind-map it.** Divide the brain dump into categories, themes or similar ideas. You can do this on a poster board with post-it notes, or a big sheet of paper with markers. You can also visit www.mindmeister.com to do an electronic mind-map.

3. **Write one chapter that is easy for you to write:** Choose the low-hanging fruit. Start with the easiest chapter you can write. Don't worry about technique, grammar, spelling, or anything. Just write and embrace the uncertainty and enjoy the mystery as you watch your writing unfold.

Divinity and Creativity

"If you bring forth what is within you, what you bring forth will save you. If you do not bring forth what is within you, what you do not bring forth will destroy you."

– Gospel of Thomas

Don't hold it in. Remember, you are on your own hero's journey. Everyone gets a "call to action" at some point in their lives. This call can be a variety of things, but this is for sure: It's something you cannot ignore.

It's a haunting. You can't shake it and you know you must do it, and if you don't do it, you will think about it until the day you die and it will be one of your greatest regrets, so why not start today? Now that you know how to break through resistance and jump over your fear and enjoy the process you will be unstoppable.

Embrace your calling as a writer. Synchronicities will occur and you will be guided. The trick is to know that you are never alone. You are always being guided by the divine and it's when you finally surrender that your greatest wins will happen.

Not surprisingly, it's in the completion of your writing that you will find the most joy. Not just because it's finished, but because there is always a great opportunity waiting on the other side.

I have had clients be offered speaking gigs, podcast interviews, and grow their businesses. I've also had clients who discovered a new part of their childhood, healed deep wounds from past trauma, and even see remarkable positive shifts in their relationships. Finishing your book will undoubtedly show you what's behind the curtain to a new life and a new way of being. Trusting the Divine to show you the way takes the pressure off because you realize you're never doing it alone, and there is a bigger picture unfolding.

Calling in Your Muse

1. There is only one way to tap into the abundant never-ending flow of the muse and that is to write at the same time each day (or close to it). Try it for one week.

2. Clichés exist because they are mostly true. Here's one to live by as a writer: pick a time to write regularly, set a timer for a short amount at first. Your mind will build the habit and it will get easier and easier.

3. In 2004 a western medicine primary care doctor told me to "light a candle and take a warm bath every night for ten days (for my anxiety), then all it will take is for you to light a candle to feel relaxed, just like the feeling in the bath." This is true for writing. It could be a candle, incense, a type of music, etc. Set up a ritual before you write each day that will trigger your mind and body to easily go into writing mode. If you do this often you can trigger your inner muse to join you at your writing desk on command.

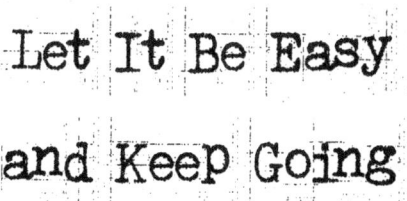

Let It Be Easy and Keep Going

Once you relax into your stillness and manage your mind, you can remain open to a journey that will look so different from what you expected, you'll be amazed at how easy your writing becomes and better than you expected. Then when you keep going and going until the end you will realize this is the best time in all of human history to be a writer.

Gone are the days where you must beg an agent or publishing company to pick you. Gone are the days where you must drive from city to city with caseloads of your book, asking bookstores if they will stock it. Gone are the days when a writer would write for weeks and months, only to have their book collect dust in the basement, read by no one.

I truly believe that God has set up the world so that writers and creatives of all kinds can finally be seen globally and make a big impact by sharing their work with the world.

We are born creators, and the art of stringing words together to tell stories require us to channel our creative selves. When we finally give in and embrace writing as a messy, confusing, exciting art, we give ourselves over to the divine. We finally learn the ultimate feeling of self-trust and courage.

You are at the right place at the right time. This is your time to shine. Armed with the tools to break through resistance, nothing can stop you.

Questions / Thoughts for Inquiry

1. Create a writing mantra in the present tense and say it every day and write it in your journal every day. I have done this for years and so far almost everything has come true. Currently mine is "I'm a healthy, happy best-selling writer who makes a difference and helps millions out of resistance to write." Yours might be something like, "I'm a healthy, joyful powerful writer who makes $10k in passive income a month from my writing" Make sure it's in the present tense and you only use words in the positive, avoid words like "don't" "can't" or "stress-free" if your stress free than you're "calm."

2. Focus on one thing at a time. Just focus on finishing. You can hire an editor later, your job is not to write well, it's to write and finish.

3. Be grateful every day for your gift of writing and for the ability to make a difference in your life and others, when you break through your resistance you unconsciously give permission for others to do the same.

In Closing

By now you should know exactly what resistance styles you have and a better understanding of how resistance is nature's way of keeping us safe. We have evolved to a place where most of our danger is imaginary and holds us back from our potential. It's important we manage our mindset and realize the consequences of how we will feel if we do not follow our purpose to write.

My hope is that you find yourself writing with ease and that you approach life with courage and confidence. And remember, breaking through resistance will help all areas of your life, not just writing. We must face our fears head on and realize we are more powerful than we thought possible.

If you have any questions along the way, please know help is always available to you. In the following section I outline different ways we can connect.

"Words are our most inexhaustible source of magic."

–J. K. Rowling

How to Get More Help

If you'd like to work with me, or know more about my offerings and writing workshops go to:

www.dawnmontefusco.com

If you'd like to know more about how to write a short book and want to have weekly Q & A with me check out my One Short Book: The New Best Seller program at:

www.oneshortbook.com

I also have a free writing group community on Facebook called, Write From Your Heart, and you can join for free at:

www.facebook.com/groups/writefromyourheart

Feel free to email me at:

dawnmontefusco@gmail.com

About the Author

Recognized as a global leader in her field, Dawn's life-changing transformative programs, speaking and events have reached more than 100,000 people in thirty countries. Dawn Montefusco, MFA, is an award-winning poet, author, speaker, Transformational Writing Coach and CEO of Inside Light Creative, LLC – a global coaching company focused on helping heart-centered, passionate writers break through creative resistance, connect to their authentic voice and share their story.

She is the author of *Write Your True Story: Unleash Your Creativity; Share Your Message and Inspire the World*; and a collection of poems titled, *Stay With Me.*

Dawn holds a degree in writing from NYU and an MFA in creative writing from Eastern Washington University. She earned her Transformational Coaching Certification from Erickson College.

Acknowledgments

First and foremost, I'd like to thank my mother. We are proof that it's possible to transform a rocky childhood into a loving relationship. Next, I'd like to thank Jenna Roberts who this book is dedicated to. She has shown me what true friendship means and her emotional support has gotten me through some of the hardest times of my adult life. She told me to keep writing and keep writing and keep writing.

I'd like to thank Shanda Trofe for her wonderful guidance and amazing team to help me publish this book. I feel blessed to work with such a wonderful woman and writer. Also, my editor Dana who is a dream to work with. Thank you for all you do.

And finally, I'd like to thank my fans, clients and students. You are the reason I do what I do, and you have been a blessing. You all allow me to live into my dream to help writers break through resistance. I love each one of you and I love that you are following your soul's purpose to write. Keep writing.